Shifty Characters
copyright © 2010 Shirley Francis-Salley and Clay Jars Publishing

This is a work of fiction, and no part of the
book or any illustrations may be used, except for
brief excerpts in a review, without written permission from

Clay Jars Publishing
2152 Ralph Avenue #414
Brooklyn, NY 11234
http://www.clayjarspublishing.com

Illustrations copyright © 2010
by Aidana WillowRaven and
Clay Jars Publishing

Book design by Aidana WillowRaven

The author can be reached via email at:
justgottawrite@aol.com

Library of Congress Control Number: 2010900976
ISBN-13: 978-0-9843369-0-6

Printed in the United States of America.

by Shirley Francis-Salley

illustrated by WillowRaven

For your own copy of the **Shifty Characters** font, look on the **Shifty Characters** Website: http://www.shiftycharacters.net

To my awesome Father God I say thank you.
To my loving and wonderfully supportive husband Joseph,
and to my dear friends Chris and Jeanine Daniels, Jaha Wilder, and Laurie Midgette,
I say thank you for your God inspired belief in my vision.

And a special thank you to my illustrator,
Aidana Willowraven
who wore many hats and held my hand from inception to fruition.

You all were the wind beneath my wings.

Letters are really cool characters.
They belong to the alphabet.
They stand beside each other
to form words we don't often forget.

When they are ready to move,
these characters know things just won't be the same.
The words they were a moment ago
are now about to change.

They switch their places for new spaces.
They like to move around,
to create new words, create new thoughts,
and to also create new sounds.

Aldo the APE
has a very large shape.
He doesn't look tall when he walks on all fours.
But, that's the way he moves around.
You'll find him mostly on the ground.

He has no tail like a monkey,
to swing from a branch in a tree.
When the letters shift places they change Aldo the APE,
Into Aldo the little green PEA.

An American Paint is a very smart horse.
It's named for its colorful coat,
of course.

You'll find it at rodeos, ranches, and races,
On nature trails
and at horse riding places.

When the letters won't horse around anymore,
They'll shift and change a HORSE to a SHORE.

Have you ever seen the inside of a barn?
It's a house for cows and hay.
You'll find other animals living there, too,
if you visit a farm one day.

The word ATE sounds like plate.
Run home for lunch and don't be late.
I know you'll tell me what you ate.
And tell me if you licked your plate.

When the letters change places,
The word ATE no longer sounds like plate.
The letters decide to shift
and be a tasty cup of ginger TEA.

Gulp down your cookies and milk.
Take two swallows, and it's all gone.
When you drink and eat your food too fast,
It doesn't last for long.

But if you take a tiny sip,
Or a bite as small as a bug,
You might not get to finish before,
The letters turn GULP into PLUG.

The word SING has a beautiful ring.
Sing Do- Re- Mi- Fa- So- La- Ti.
But when the letters change their position,

They have a new meaning; they have a new mission.
They change what was SING into a SIGN,
To tell you where hungry people might dine.

Loop, loop, loop, and dive,
Are tricks a pilot can do,
He turns his plane upside down.
Wow, isn't that really cool?

But oh, watch out for the letters!
They're about to make a move.
You had better grab a swimsuit. Quick!
For they've changed a LOOP to a POOL.

A sole has an important job: It's the bottom part of your shoe.
It protects your feet from nails and glass.
And rocks and pebbles, too.

But there's one thing I must tell you.
I must give you this news.

When the letters start to move around,
your SOLE you are going to LOSE.

And when your SOLE is changed
to LOSE, don't let it get you down.

You'll find your sole the next time
that the letters move around.

Inch by inch is how we measure
the length of something that grows.
It could be your kitten's tail.
It could even be your nose.

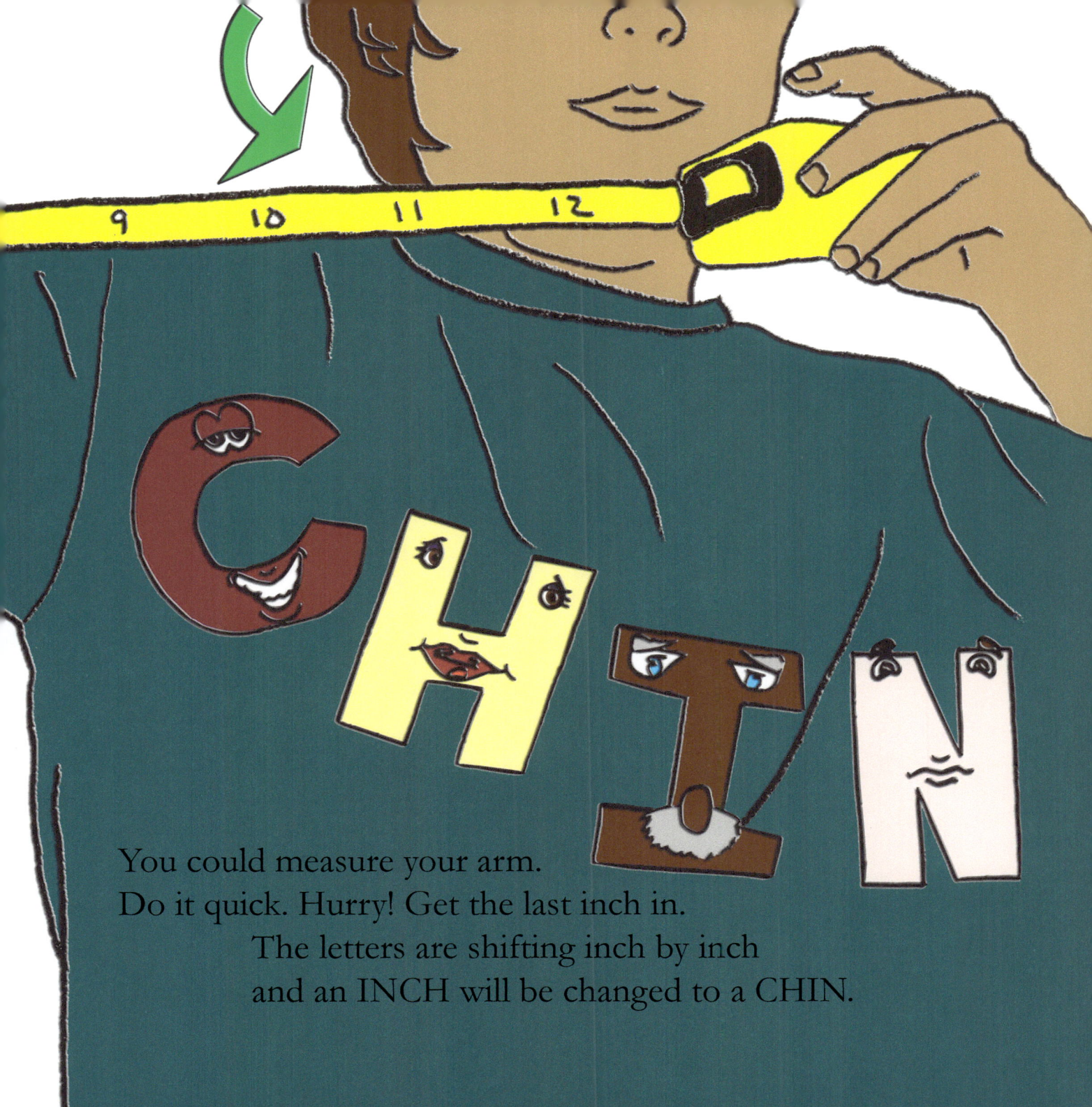

You could measure your arm.
Do it quick. Hurry! Get the last inch in.
The letters are shifting inch by inch
and an INCH will be changed to a CHIN.

The word cheap means
   something does not cost a lot.
      You might be able to buy what you want,
         With the sixty-five cents that you've got,
            You can't buy a slice of pizza,
               Because pizza is not that cheap,

But wait just a moment, the letters have changed.
The word that was CHEAP is now PEACH.

Shifty Characters love to move. They won't stand still for long.
They are always changing and rearranging,
Until the word that was there is gone.

And that's the way God works with us, for we are characters, too.
We need to be changed and rearranged
To make our lives brand new.

Characters are often grownups,
but sometimes they're children, too.
Here are some types of characters that might be familiar to you.

Some characters like to fight; some characters like to tell lies.
Some characters like to be mean and rude;
They like to make others cry.

They don't obey their parents or the teachers at their schools.
They're rough and tough; they're bullies.
They don't care about the rules.

But God can
change these characters
with His Spirit,
His Holy Wind.
He'll get inside
of their hearts and minds,
and something
new will begin.

Fighting will change to
caring and sharing;
rude and mean
will change to kind.
Disobeying and
trouble-making
will be left behind.

These kinds of changes can happen when we join God's family.
He can change the way we act and live, and everyone will see,

God and His Holy Spirit have filled our hearts with love,
And Jesus is watching over us from His home in Heaven above.

Author ~ Shirley Francis-Salley

Shirley Francis-Salley is a children's ministry teacher and award winning author. For more than ten years she has been dedicated to a mission of creating Sunday school lessons that make the word of God appealing and practical in the daily lives of children in grades K-6. Her love of children and writing led her to do field writing for a few well known Christian publishers including Cook Communications Ministries. She has published articles, short stories, skits, Bible dramas, song lyrics, board games, Sunday school lessons and lesson plans.

As a wife, mother, grandma, teacher and writer, she has countless opportunities to talk about the situations of everyday life that confront us no matter what age we are. Shirley resides in New York with her husband Joseph and their cat, Shadow.

Illustrator ~ Aidana WillowRaven

Aidana WillowRaven, mother of three, was trained in Fine Art, Studio Design and Animation at Norfolk State and Old Dominion universities.

She has illustrated and/or designed over forty-five books through her company, WillowRaven Illustration & Design Plus, in Tennessee.

View samples or contact her through her website:

http://WillowRaven.weebly.com

www.ingramcontent.com/pod-product-compliance
Lightning Source LLC
Chambersburg PA
CBHW041201290426
44109CB00002B/87